DECORATED
Whoopie Pies

Text and Photography by

ELISABETH ANTOINE AND ELIZABETH CUNNINGHAM HERRING

SELLERS
PUBLISHING

To Paco, Nane, Yves, Mony, and Anne-Marie
for their unwavering love and support.
—Elisabeth Antoine

To Dick, Budgy, Caroline, and Richard
for their love and encouragement.
—Elizabeth Cunningham Herring

Acknowledgments

*We would like to thank our families and friends for their support and for
tasting and helping us refine our recipes. We are particularly grateful
to Caroline Cunningham for her patient and gracious advice.*

*We would also like to thank the crew at Sellers Publishing,
especially Robin Haywood, Jeff Hall, and Charlotte Cromwell.*

Published by Sellers Publishing, Inc.

Text and photography copyright © 2013 Elisabeth Antoine & Elizabeth Cunningham Herring
All rights reserved.

Sellers Publishing, Inc.
161 John Roberts Road, South Portland, Maine 04106
Visit our Web site: www.sellerspublishing.com
E-mail: rsp@rsvp.com

ISBN 13: 978-1-4162-0886-0
e-ISBN: 978-1-4162-0904-1
Library of Congress Control Number: 2012944702

10 9 8 7 6 5 4 3 2 1

Printed and bound in China.

Contents

Introduction 4

Materials and Techniques 6

Fondant Fundamentals 15

Unidentified Flying Whoopie 17

Sunny Side Up 25

It's a Dog's Life 33

Something Borrowed, Something Blue . . . 41

Itsy Bitsy Spiders 49

A Big Frog in a Small Pond 57

Ladybug, Ladybug 65

A Not-So-Hungry Caterpillar 73

With This Ring . . . 81

Sweet Baby Dreams 89

Monster and Co. 97

Flower Power 105

Funny Faces 113

Holiday Stockings 121

Table of Equivalents 128

W hat do you get when you cross a cookie with a cupcake and fill it with frosting like an ice-cream sandwich? A whoopie pie, of course! Coming in a delightful assortment of flavors, whoopie pies epitomize fun.

Though the origins of these delectable treats are debatable, most agree that they were invented by Amish farmers in the early 20th century. Leftover cake batter was used to create the treats, which were neat, compact, and easily transported in a lunch box. Apparently when children spied them they would shout "whoopie!"

Whoopie pies are surprisingly simple to make. While special whoopie-pie pans are available, it's just as easy and effective to use a parchment-covered cookie sheet. Included in the Materials and Techniques section that opens the book are step-by-step directions accompanied by detailed photographs for both options, making the process as easy as whoopie pie!

The traditional whoopie-pie recipe consists of a chocolate cake filled with marshmallow frosting, but like its cupcake cousin, the whoopie pie is highly adaptable to lots of different flavors. Each chapter includes a unique, simple-to-make, and delicious recipe combination. Feel free to experiment with different flavor combinations by mixing and matching the recipes.

Not only are they delicious, but whoopie pies are also aesthetically appealing, as both the cake and frosting are visible, creating a yummy and often quite colorful contrast.

In addition, the gently curved top of the whoopie pie makes a wonderful canvas for decorating. Each chapter features detailed instructions on how to create unique designs out of fondant, a versatile, sugar-based substance that is often used to cover wedding and other specialty cakes. There are adorable characters as well as memorable decorations to suit every occasion.

While they can be made in advance to serve at any celebration, these decorated whoopie pies can also serve as the party activity. Children and adults alike will delight in crafting these colorful and entertaining whoopie-pie toppers.

It's a funny thing, but just try to say "whoopie pie" without smiling. Then gather up your ingredients and get ready to cook up some fun!

Nothing says fun like a plate of whoopie pies. And they are surprisingly simple to make.

All the recipes in this book have been designed so that the whoopie pies will rise on a cookie sheet. No special pans are required. However, if you like, you can use a special whoopie-pie pan, which you can find easily in your local kitchen-supply or craft store. We like to keep things simple, so we used the cookie sheet for all the whoopie-pie recipes. We also prefer the look of a whoopie pie made on a cookie sheet — it's a bit flatter and so lends itself better to decorating. In the following pages, we've included simple instructions using both options.

While the recipes in this book all feature a fondant decoration on top and detailed instructions on how to make it, there are plenty of simpler ways to decorate whoopie pies. At the end of this section, you will find some easy and colorful decorating ideas.

You will need

- Prepared cake batter in a large bowl
- Wooden spoon
- Large or small ice-cream scoop
- Parchment paper
- Cookie sheet or whoopie-pie pan
- Spoon (if using whoopie-pie pan)
- Butter to grease whoopie-pie pan
- Teaspoon
- Knife to spread frosting
- Resealable plastic bag
- Scissors

Optional Items

- Food coloring
- Toppings (nuts, chocolate shavings, sprinkles, glitter, or coconut)
- Confectioners' sugar or cocoa (for dusting)
- Chocolate or colored candy coating
- Edible flowers
- Fondant
- Mini fondant cutters

1.

Prepare the whoopie-pie batter according to the chosen recipe.

2.

Use an ice-cream scoop to place equal-sized mounds of batter about 3 inches apart on a parchment-lined cookie sheet. The scoops come in a wide range of sizes — most of the whoopie pies in this book were made using a small-sized scoop (about ⅓ of the volume of a regular ice-cream scoop).

3.

You can also use a whoopie-pie pan. Grease the pan with butter and simply spoon the batter into the cups until they are ¾ full. These will be more uniform than the ones made on the cookie sheet. However, they will also be thicker and will not have the traditional whoopie-pie shape.

4.

Follow the baking instructions in the recipe. Let the whoopie pies cool completely before adding the filling. You can use a knife to spread the filling on top of a whoopie-pie half. Place another whoopie half on top to create a sandwich.

5.

For a neater appearance, you can choose to pipe the whoopie-pie filling. Place the filling in a resealable plastic bag and cut out a small corner.

6.

Use 2 hands to firmly squeeze the bag and pipe the filling around the edge of the whoopie half, finishing in the middle.

7.

Place the other half of the whoopie on top and gently press. The whoopie pie on the left was made on a cookie sheet. The one on the right was made in a whoopie-pie pan.

8.

Because you can see both the cake and the frosting together, whoopie pies are very attractive on their own, but they have an added wow factor when decorated. There are so many easy ways to decorate them.

9.

Adding a few drops of food coloring to the frosting is a simple way to jazz up a whoopie pie.

10.

Here is an example of whoopie pies with 3 different-colored fillings.

11.

Rolling the edges of the frosting in a topping such as nuts, chocolate shavings, sprinkles, or coconut adds texture, flavor, and visual interest.

12.

You can dust the top of the whoopie pie with confectioners' sugar or cocoa. You can also use a simple stencil made with parchment paper to create a shape on the whoopie pie.

13.

To add a drizzle, melt a little chocolate or candy coating in the microwave in a resealable plastic bag. Snip off a small corner and squeeze the bag to create whatever pattern you like.

14.

You can also melt the chocolate or candy coating in a small bowl and dip part of the whoopie pie in it. You can then add sprinkles, glitter, or any topping you choose before the dipped part sets.

15.

Premade edible flowers or other decorations can be found in your local craft store. They can be used on their own or in conjunction with drizzle for a professional look.

16.

Covering the top of the whoopie pie with fondant is another good option. Craft stores sell a variety of mini fondant cutters, which you can use to create simple and cute decorations.

A key ingredient in many wedding and other specialty cakes, fondant is a truly amazing substance. This sweet concoction was used to create the whoopie-pie toppers in this book.

We recommend that you use commercial fondant, which can be found in your local cake-supply or craft store. We suggest that you purchase white fondant and use food coloring to achieve the desired shade.

Following are some tips to follow when working with fondant:

- After adding food coloring, knead the fondant until the color is evenly blended. If you use gel food coloring (our product of choice), you may want to wear plastic gloves during this process to avoid rainbow-colored hands. (Once the food coloring is thoroughly mixed with the fondant, you won't have to worry.) It is better to make a little more of a color than you think you'll need, as it may be hard to match the color later.

- You may want to use a tiny bit of water to "glue" pieces of fondant together. For example, if you need to affix an eye to a figure and it doesn't stick properly, dip a toothpick in some water and use it to "glue" the eye on.

- When not working with the fondant, place it in a resealable plastic bag or airtight container until you are ready to use it. If stored properly at room temperature, commercial fondant will last for 18 months.

- The fondant toppers can be made up to 2 days ahead. Store them in a cake-storage container or a lightly covered tray at room temperature. They should be kept in a cool, dry place.

- Never put the fondant toppers in the refrigerator or freezer, as this will cause the toppers to get soft and shiny. You should also avoid storing the finished fondant toppers in an airtight bag or container, as this will have a similar effect. It's important that air circulates, so that the finished fondant figures are able to dry and harden.

Unidentified Flying Whoopie

Chocolate Brownie Whoopie Pies with Mint Buttercream Filling

Who would believe that an alien invasion could be this tasty? Youngsters looking for a fun party activity and scrumptious treat will find themselves lost in space over these yummy U.F.W.s!

Makes about 8–9 large whoopie pies or 18–20 small ones.

INGREDIENTS

For the Whoopie Pies

½ cup unsalted butter, softened

1½ cups sugar

2 large eggs

½ cup milk

1 tablespoon vanilla extract

2 cups all-purpose flour

6 tablespoons unsweetened cocoa powder

2 teaspoons baking powder

1 teaspoon baking soda

Pinch of salt

1½ cups semisweet mini chocolate chips

For the Filling

1 cup unsalted butter, softened

4 cups confectioners' sugar

6 drops peppermint oil

3 drops green food coloring

Preheat oven to 350°F (180°C). Grease 2 cookie sheets with butter or cover them with parchment paper.

For the Whoopie Pies

In a large bowl, mix together butter and sugar. Add eggs and then milk and vanilla and mix well. In a medium bowl, mix together flour, cocoa powder, baking powder, baking soda, and salt. Add the flour mixture to the butter mixture and stir gently with a wooden spoon until just combined. Add mini chocolate chips.

With an ice-cream scoop or spoon, scoop the batter onto the cookie sheet, making sure to leave 3 inches between each whoopie. Bake in the center of the oven for about 15 minutes or until the top of a whoopie pie springs back when lightly pressed down. Cool on a rack for 30 minutes before filling. Store unfilled whoopie pies in a resealable container at room temperature or in the refrigerator for up to 3 days.

For the Filling

In a large bowl, cream butter with an electric mixer. Gradually add sugar, beating well and scraping the sides of the bowl. Add peppermint oil and food coloring and beat until light and fluffy. Store in the refrigerator until ready to fill the whoopie pies. If the filling gets too hard, let it sit out at room temperature until it's soft enough to pipe or spread. The filling can be stored in a resealable container in the refrigerator for up to 2 days.

See pages 8–10 for filling instructions.

You will need

- Fondant in the following colors: gray, light blue, red, yellow
- Rolling pin
- Parchment paper
- Sharp knife
- Toothpick

1.

Assemble the whoopie pie (see pages 8–10 for instructions).

2.

With the rolling pin, flatten a large ball of gray fondant on a sheet of parchment paper. Use the sharp knife to cut a circle slightly larger than the whoopie pie.

3.

Place the gray fondant circle on top of the whoopie pie.

4.

Use the sharp knife and the toothpick to make indentations on the gray fondant to create a riveted-metal look as shown.

5.

With light-blue fondant, roll a medium-sized ball in your hands and flatten one end to create a half sphere.

6.

Apply the half sphere to the center of the gray fondant to create the glass top of the U.F.W.

Roll a tiny ball of red fondant and apply it to the top of the light-blue fondant.

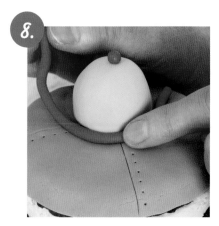

Roll a small amount of red fondant into a long, thin, sausage-like shape and apply it to the base of the light-blue fondant as shown.

9.

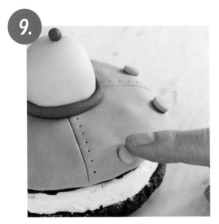

With yellow fondant, make 8 tiny balls, flatten and apply them as shown to create the U.F.W.'s landing lights.

10.

With gray fondant, create 4 cylinder-shaped legs and apply them to the edge of the U.F.W. as shown. With red fondant, make 4 little balls for feet and apply them to the legs as shown.

Sunny Side Up

Lemon Poppy Whoopie Pies with Lemon Curd Buttercream Filling

Turn your savory breakfast into a sweet one with this egg-and-bacon whoopie pie. What a happy way to greet the day!

Makes about 8–9 large whoopie pies or 18–20 small ones.

INGREDIENTS

For the Whoopie Pies

½ cup unsalted butter, softened

1 cup sugar

1 large egg

2 tablespoons lemon zest

2 cups all-purpose flour

2 teaspoons baking powder

⅛ teaspoon salt

½ cup buttermilk

1 teaspoon poppy seeds

For the Filling

1 cup unsalted butter, softened

4 cups confectioners' sugar

1 teaspoon vanilla extract

4 teaspoons lemon curd

2 teaspoons fresh lemon juice

1 teaspoon lemon zest

Preheat oven to 350°F (180°C). Grease 2 cookie sheets with butter or cover them with parchment paper.

For the Whoopie Pies

In a large bowl, mix together butter and sugar. Add egg and then lemon zest and mix well. In a medium bowl, mix together flour, baking powder, and salt. Add about half the flour mixture to the butter/sugar mixture, and then add buttermilk, and then the rest of the flour mixture. Stir gently with a wooden spoon until well blended. Add poppy seeds.

With an ice-cream scoop or spoon, scoop the batter onto the cookie sheet, making sure to leave 3 inches between each whoopie. Bake in the center of the oven for about 15 minutes or until the top of a whoopie pie springs back when lightly pressed down. Cool on a rack for 30 minutes before filling. Store unfilled whoopie pies in a resealable container at room temperature or in the refrigerator for up to 3 days.

For the Filling

In a large bowl, cream butter with an electric mixer. Gradually add sugar, beating well and scraping the sides of the bowl. Add vanilla, lemon curd, lemon juice, and lemon zest and beat until light and fluffy. Store in the refrigerator until ready to fill the whoopie pies. If the filling gets too hard, let it sit out at room temperature until it's soft enough to pipe or spread. The filling can be stored in a resealable container in the refrigerator for up to 2 days.

See pages 8–10 for filling instructions.

You will need

- Fondant in the following colors: white, yellow, light tan, brownish red
- Rolling pin
- Parchment paper
- Sharp knife

1.

Assemble the whoopie pie (see pages 8–10 for instructions).

2.

With the rolling pin, flatten a large ball of white fondant on a sheet of parchment paper.

Use the sharp knife to cut an irregular shape (like a fried egg) roughly the same size as the top of the whoopie pie.

Place the white-fondant egg on top of the whoopie pie.

5.

Roll a medium-sized ball of yellow fondant and flatten one side to create a half sphere. This will be the egg yolk.

6.

Place the egg yolk in the center of the white fondant on the top of the whoopie pie.

7.

With light-tan fondant, create 3 strips, each of irregular thickness as shown.

8.

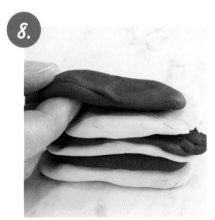

Repeat the same process using brownish-red fondant. Stack the 6 strips, alternating colors as shown. Press the layers together slightly.

9.

Use the sharp knife to cut slices of "bacon," trimming the ends and shaping the pieces in a wavy manner as shown.

10.

Place the bacon on the egg as shown. Breakfast is ready!

It's a Dog's Life

Carrot Cake Whoopie Pies with Cinnamon Spice Buttercream Filling

Nestled in his soft bed with a new bone by his side, this pup is living like a top dog. This easy-to-make "woofie" pie is sure to have dog-loving fans barking for more.

Makes about 8–9 large whoopie pies or 18–20 small ones.

INGREDIENTS

For the Whoopie Pies

$^1/_2$ cup vegetable oil

1 cup sugar

1 large egg

1 teaspoon vanilla extract

2 cups all-purpose flour

2 teaspoons baking powder

$^1/_4$ teaspoon salt

$1^1/_2$ teaspoons cinnamon

$^1/_8$ teaspoon nutmeg

$^1/_2$ cup buttermilk

1 cup carrots, peeled and shredded

For the Filling

1 cup unsalted butter, softened

4 cups confectioners' sugar

1 teaspoon vanilla extract

2 teaspoons milk

2 teaspoons cinnamon

Preheat oven to 350°F (180°C). Grease 2 cookie sheets with butter or cover them with parchment paper.

For the Whoopie Pies

In a large bowl, mix together vegetable oil and sugar. Add egg and then vanilla and mix well. In a medium bowl, mix together flour, baking powder, salt, cinnamon, and nutmeg. Add about half the flour mixture to the vegetable oil/sugar mixture, and then add buttermilk, and then the rest of the flour mixture. Stir gently with a wooden spoon until well blended. Carefully fold in carrots.

With an ice-cream scoop or spoon, scoop the batter onto the cookie sheet, making sure to leave 3 inches between each whoopie. Bake in the center of the oven for about 15 minutes or until the top of a whoopie pie springs back when lightly pressed down. Cool on a rack for 30 minutes before filling. Store unfilled whoopie pies in a resealable container at room temperature or in the refrigerator for up to 3 days.

For the Filling

In a large bowl, cream butter with an electric mixer. Gradually add sugar, beating well and scraping the sides of the bowl. Add vanilla, milk, and cinnamon and beat until light and fluffy. Store in the refrigerator until ready to fill the whoopie pies. If the filling gets too hard, let it sit out at room temperature until it's soft enough to pipe or spread. The filling can be stored in a resealable container in the refrigerator for up to 2 days.

See pages 8–10 for filling instructions.

- Fondant in the following colors: tan, brown, white, black
- Rolling pin
- Parchment paper
- Sharp knife

1.

Assemble the whoopie pie (see pages 8–10 for instructions).

2.

With the rolling pin, flatten a large ball of tan fondant on a sheet of parchment paper. Use the sharp knife to cut a circle slightly smaller than the top of the whoopie pie.

3.

Roll a smaller piece of tan fondant into a sausage-like shape and place it along the edge of the circle to create a dog bed. Then place the bed on top of the whoopie pie as shown.

4.

With some brown fondant, form a 3-inch cylinder (the dog's body) and slit one end as shown to create the dog's front legs.

5. Place the dog's body in the bed as shown and add a little piece of brown fondant to form the tail.

6. With a small piece of brown fondant, shape the back leg and place it on the dog as shown.

7.

With a small piece of brown fondant, form a cone to create the dog's head and place it on the dog's body as shown.

8.

Create the dog's eyes by placing teensy dots of black fondant on tiny balls of white fondant. Flatten the eyes slightly and place them on the head as shown.

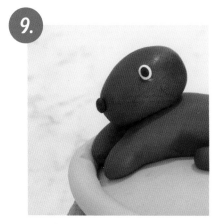

9.

Roll a tiny ball of black fondant and flatten to create the dog's nose and place it on the dog's head as shown.

10.

With brown fondant, create long ears and affix one to each side of the dog's head as shown. Use a small amount of white fondant to create a bone shape and place it on the bed next to the dog.

Something Borrowed, Something Blue . . .

Coconut Cake Whoopie Pies with Vanilla Buttercream Filling
Rolled in Coconut Flakes

Good things come in small packages, especially when the box is
Tiffany blue like the one shown here. Perfect for bridal showers, this
elegant little gift tastes as good as it looks.

Makes about 8–9 large whoopie pies or 18–20 small ones.

INGREDIENTS

For the Whoopie Pies

½ cup vegetable oil
1 cup light brown sugar,
  firmly packed
2 large eggs, separated
1 teaspoon coconut extract
½ cup sour cream
2 cups all-purpose flour
1 teaspoon baking soda
2 teaspoons baking powder
Pinch of salt
2 cups sweetened coconut
  flakes, separated

For the Filling

1 cup unsalted butter,
  softened
1 teaspoon vanilla extract
4 cups confectioners' sugar
2 teaspoons milk

Preheat oven to 350°F (180°C). Grease 2 cookie sheets with
butter or cover them with parchment paper.

For the Whoopie Pies

In a large bowl, mix together vegetable oil and sugar. Add egg yolks and then coconut extract and sour cream and mix well. In a medium bowl, mix together flour, baking soda, baking powder, and salt. Add the flour mixture to the batter. Stir gently with a wooden spoon until just combined. In a small bowl, beat egg whites until stiff peaks form. Gently fold egg whites into the batter. Carefully fold in 1 cup coconut flakes.

With an ice-cream scoop or spoon, scoop the batter onto the cookie sheet, making sure to leave 3 inches between each whoopie. Bake in the center of the oven for about 11–14 minutes or until the top of a whoopie pie springs back when lightly pressed down. Cool on a rack for 30 minutes before filling. Store unfilled whoopie pies in a resealable container at room temperature or in the refrigerator for up to 3 days.

For the Filling

In a large bowl, cream butter with an electric mixer. Add vanilla and then gradually add sugar, beating well and scraping the sides of the bowl. Add milk and beat until light and fluffy. Store in the refrigerator until ready to fill the whoopie pies. If the filling gets too hard, let it sit out at room temperature until it's soft enough to pipe or spread. The filling can be stored in a resealable container in the refrigerator for up to 2 days.

See pages 8–10 for filling instructions.

1.

Assemble the whoopie pie (see pages 8–10 for instructions).

2.

Roll the sides in the remaining 1 cup coconut flakes.

3.

With the rolling pin, flatten a large ball of light-blue fondant on a sheet of parchment paper.

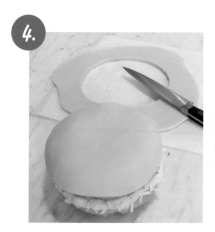

4.

Use the sharp knife to cut a circle slightly larger than the top of the whoopie pie and place it on top of the whoopie pie.

5. Roll a piece of white fondant into a long, thin, sausage-like shape. Its length should be about twice the diameter of the whoopie pie.

6. Flatten the sausage-shaped white fondant with your fingers or the rolling pin and place it across the whoopie pie. Tuck each end under the bottom of the whoopie pie as shown.

7.

Using the same technique as steps 5–6, make another strip and place it as shown.

8.

Roll and flatten a third strip (this one should be about 4 inches in length) and cut it in half. Cut a triangle at the end of each half as shown. Place the 2 halves at the center of the whoopie pie to form the ends of the bow as shown.

9.

Prepare another strip (this one 5 inches in length) and fold each end into the center as shown to form the bow. Pinch the sides by the center as shown.

10.

Prepare a 2-inch strip, slightly narrower than the others, and tuck it around the center of the bow as shown. Place the bow on the package.

Itsy Bitsy Spiders

Devil's Food Whoopie Pies with 7-Minute Filling

Don't worry if you get caught in these spiders' webs. You can eat your way out of danger! Serve these spooky little guys at your next Halloween party.

Makes about 10–12 large whoopie pies or 22–24 small ones.

INGREDIENTS

For the Whoopie Pies

$^{1}/_{2}$ cup unsalted butter

3 ounces unsweetened chocolate

1$^{1}/_{2}$ cups dark brown sugar, firmly packed

1 large egg

1 teaspoon vanilla extract

2 cups all-purpose flour

1$^{1}/_{2}$ teaspoons baking soda

$^{1}/_{4}$ teaspoon salt

$^{3}/_{4}$ cup buttermilk

For the Filling

1$^{3}/_{4}$ cups sugar

$^{1}/_{2}$ cup water

4 egg whites at room temperature

$^{1}/_{2}$ teaspoon cream of tartar

1 teaspoon vanilla extract

Preheat oven to 350°F (180°C). Grease 2 cookie sheets with butter or cover them with parchment paper.

For the Whoopie Pies

Melt butter and chocolate together in a double boiler. In a large bowl, stir together the melted chocolate mixture and sugar. Add egg and vanilla and mix until well blended. In a medium bowl, mix together flour, baking soda, and salt. Add about half the flour mixture to the chocolate batter, and then add buttermilk, and then the rest of the flour mixture. Stir gently with a wooden spoon until well blended.

With an ice-cream scoop or spoon, scoop the batter onto the cookie sheet, making sure to leave 3 inches between each whoopie. Bake in the center of the oven for about 14 minutes or until the top of a whoopie pie springs back when lightly pressed down. Cool on a rack for 30 minutes before filling. Store unfilled whoopie pies in a resealable container at room temperature or in the refrigerator for up to 3 days.

For the Filling

Mix sugar and water in a saucepan and bring to a boil. Let boil for 3 to 4 minutes or until a candy thermometer registers 242°F (117°C). In a large bowl, beat egg whites and cream of tartar with an electric mixer at high speed until frothy. Slowly add the sugar mixture to the egg whites and continue to beat on high for 5 minutes or until soft peaks form. Add vanilla and continue beating until filling reaches desired consistency. Store in the refrigerator until ready to fill the whoopie pies. If the filling gets too hard, let it sit out at room temperature until it's soft enough to pipe or spread. The filling can be stored in a resealable container in the refrigerator for up to 2 days. See pages 8–10 for filling instructions.

- White candy coating for drizzling
- Fondant in the following colors: red, white, black
- Rolling pin
- Parchment paper
- Sharp knife

1.

Assemble the whoopie pie (see pages 8–10 for instructions).

2.

With the rolling pin, flatten a large ball of red fondant on a sheet of parchment paper. Use the sharp knife to cut a circle slightly larger than the top of the whoopie pie and place it on top of the whoopie pie.

3. Chop a small amount of white candy coating and place it in a small resealable plastic bag. Seal it and microwave on low until the coating is melted. Use scissors to cut a very small piece of the bag's corner. (You can also use a pastry bag.)

4. Pipe the candy coating on top of the red fondant in a spiderweb pattern as shown. Set aside and let dry for 30 minutes.

5.

Roll a small ball of black fondant to form the spider's body.

6.

Roll a small, olive-shaped ball of black fondant to form the spider's head. Use a sharp knife to create a horizontal mouth opening as shown. Attach the head to the spider's body as shown.

7. Use white fondant to create 2 tiny eyeballs and place them where the head meets the body as shown. Use black fondant to create 2 teensy pupils and place them on the eyeballs.

8. Use black fondant to create 6 1½-inch sausage-like legs and 2 1-inch legs.

9.

Place the legs on the web, posing them as shown, with the 2 short legs in the front.

10.

Place the spider's body on top of the legs as shown.

A Big Frog in a Small Pond

Red Velvet Whoopie Pies with Cream Cheese Filling

Could there be anything sweeter than a spotted frog perched on a lily-pad whoopie pie? Crafting this little guy would make a wonderful and delicious rainy-day activity.

Makes about 8–9 large whoopie pies or 18–20 small ones.

INGREDIENTS

For the Whoopie Pies

2 cups all-purpose flour

3 tablespoons unsweetened cocoa powder

1 teaspoon baking soda

Pinch of salt

2 large eggs

1 cup sour cream

1 cup light brown sugar, firmly packed

1/2 cup vegetable oil

1 tablespoon vanilla extract

1 tablespoon red food coloring

1 1/2 teaspoons apple cider vinegar

For the Filling

1 8-ounce package cream cheese, softened

1/4 cup butter, softened

1 teaspoon vanilla extract

1 1/4 cup confectioners' sugar

Preheat oven to 375°F (190°C). Grease 2 cookie sheets with butter or cover them with parchment paper.

For the Whoopie Pies

In a medium bowl, mix together flour, cocoa powder, baking soda, and salt. In a large bowl, mix together eggs, sour cream, and sugar. Add vegetable oil, vanilla, food coloring, and apple cider vinegar and mix well. Add the flour mix to the batter and stir with a wooden spoon until just combined.

With an ice-cream scoop or spoon, scoop the batter onto the cookie sheet, making sure to leave 3 inches between each whoopie. Bake in the center of the oven for about 13 minutes or until the top of a whoopie pie springs back when lightly pressed down. Cool on a rack for 30 minutes before filling. Store unfilled whoopie pies in a resealable container at room temperature or in the refrigerator for up to 3 days.

For the Filling

In a large bowl, beat together cream cheese and butter until smooth. Add vanilla and then gradually beat in sugar.

Store in the refrigerator until ready to fill the whoopie pies. If the filling gets too hard, let it sit out at room temperature until it's soft enough to pipe or spread. The filling can be stored in a resealable container in the refrigerator for up to 2 days.

See pages 8–10 for filling instructions.

- Fondant in the following colors: blue, dark green, pink, light green, white, black
- Rolling pin
- Parchment paper
- Sharp knife
- Toothpick

1.

Assemble the whoopie pie (see pages 8–10 for instructions).

2.

With the rolling pin, flatten a large ball of blue fondant on a sheet of parchment paper. Use the sharp knife to cut a circle slightly larger than the top of the whoopie pie and place it on top of the whoopie pie.

3. Roll out some dark-green fondant and then use the knife to cut out a lily pad shape as shown. Make 3 indentations on the leaf with the knife to create the veins as shown. Apply the leaf to the top of the whoopie pie as shown.

4. Roll out a small amount of pink fondant and then use the knife to cut a triangle with a wide base. Make slits as shown and roll the base onto itself to create the lily. Press the flower onto the recessed part of the lily pad as shown.

With light-green fondant, create a small pyramid shape.

Use the knife to create a mouth. Add little spots of dark-green fondant to the frog as shown.

Place the frog on the lily pad. Use white fondant to create 2 tiny eyeballs. Use black fondant to create two teensy pupils and place them on the eyeballs. Place the eyes at the top of the frog as shown.

Flatten a tiny ball of light-green fondant and cut it in half to create eyelids. Apply each lid to the top of the frog's eyeballs.

9.

To create the back legs, roll 2 identical sausage shapes (about ¾ inch in length) with light-green fondant as shown. Fold each shape in half and attach the legs to the sides of the frog's body.

10.

To create the feet, roll out some light-green fondant and cut 4 identical triangles. Attach the feet to the frog as shown and use the toothpick to make little indentations for the toes.

Ladybug, Ladybug

Pistachio Whoopie Pie with Rose Buttercream Filling

These red and black-spotted ladybugs are super cute and super easy to make. Since the sophisticated flavors in the featured recipes may appeal more to adults, feel free to substitute a more child-friendly recipe such as devil's food.

Makes about 8–9 large whoopie pies or 18–20 small ones.

INGREDIENTS

For the Whoopie Pies

2 cups all-purpose flour

1½ teaspoons baking powder

¼ teaspoon salt

½ teaspoon cardamom powder

½ cup unsalted butter, softened

1 cup sugar

½ cup dark brown sugar, firmly packed

1 egg

1 teaspoon vanilla extract

¾ cup buttermilk

¾ cup ground pistachios

For the Filling

1 cup unsalted butter, softened

4 cups confectioners' sugar

4 teaspoons rose water (available from a gourmet- or specialty-food store)

1 drop red food coloring (optional)

Preheat oven to 350°F (180°C). Grease 2 cookie sheets with butter or cover them with parchment paper.

For the Whoopie Pies

In a medium bowl, mix together flour, baking powder, salt, and cardamom. Set aside. In a large bowl, mix together butter, both sugars, egg, and vanilla. Stir together until well blended. Add about half the flour mixture to the batter and then add buttermilk, and then the rest of the flour mixture. Fold in pistachios.

With a small ice-cream scoop or spoon, scoop the batter onto the cookie sheet, making sure to leave 3 inches between each whoopie. Bake in the center of the oven for about 12 minutes or until the top of a whoopie pie springs back when lightly pressed down. Cool on a rack for 30 minutes before filling. Store unfilled whoopie pies in a resealable container at room temperature or in the refrigerator for up to 3 days.

For the Filling

In a large bowl, cream butter with an electric mixer. Gradually add sugar, beating well and scraping the sides of the bowl. Add rose water and beat until light and fluffy. If desired, add a drop of red food coloring to the filling. Store in the refrigerator until ready to fill the whoopie pies. If the filling gets too hard, let it sit out at room temperature until it's soft enough to pipe or spread. The filling can be stored in a resealable container in the refrigerator for up to 2 days.

See pages 8–10 for filling instructions.

- Fondant in the following colors: black, red, white, pink
- Rolling pin
- Parchment paper
- Sharp knife

1.

Assemble the whoopie pie (see pages 8–10 for instructions).

2.

With the rolling pin, flatten a large ball of black fondant on a sheet of parchment paper.

3.

Use the sharp knife to cut a circle slightly larger than the top of the whoopie pie.

4.

Place the black fondant circle on top of the whoopie pie.

5.

With red fondant, make a small ball and flatten it until it is thin and round.

6.

Cut the red circle in half and pull the 2 sides apart, and then cut a small piece off the ends as shown (to form the wings).

7. Place the red wings on the black fondant as shown. Roll tiny balls of black fondant to make spots. Flatten the spots and place them around the red wings as shown.

8. For the eyes, roll 2 tiny balls of white fondant, flatten them slightly, and then place them on the black fondant as shown. Add teensy black pupils.

9.

For the nose, roll a tiny ball of pink fondant and place it as shown.

10.

With black fondant, roll a thin sausage shape and cut 2 identical sections (about ½ inch each). Add a little ball of black fondant on the end of each segment and apply the antennas to the ladybug's head as shown.

A Not-So-Hungry Caterpillar

Mango Whoopie Pie with Mango Buttercream Filling

These charming little orange-and-red caterpillars are chomping away. Who knows? By the time they get to the exotic mango cake and filling beneath the leaves, they may have transformed into beautiful butterflies.

Makes about 9–10 large whoopie pies or 18–20 small ones.

INGREDIENTS

For the Whoopie Pies

2 cups all-purpose flour

2 teaspoons baking powder

1 teaspoon baking soda

Pinch of salt

1/2 cup unsalted butter, softened

1 cup light brown sugar, firmly packed

2 large eggs, separated

1 teaspoon vanilla extract

1/2 cup sour cream

1 cup peeled, finely diced mango flesh

For the Filling

1 cup unsalted butter, softened

1 teaspoon vanilla extract

4 cups confectioners' sugar

2 tablespoons mango nectar or juice

2/3 cup pulverized freeze-dried mango (available at gourmet- or speciality-food stores or online)

Preheat oven to 350°F (180°C). Grease 2 cookie sheets with butter or cover them with parchment paper.

For the Whoopie Pies

In a medium bowl, mix together flour, baking powder, baking soda, and salt. Set aside. In a large bowl, mix together butter and sugar. Add egg yolks and vanilla and mix well. Add sour cream and stir together until well blended. Add the flour mixture to the batter and stir with a wooden spoon until just combined. In a separate bowl, beat egg whites with an electric mixer at high speed until soft peaks form. Gently fold the egg whites into the batter. Fold in the diced mango.

With a small ice-cream scoop or spoon, scoop the batter onto the cookie sheet, making sure to leave 3 inches between each whoopie. Bake in the center of the oven for about 12–14 minutes or until the top of a whoopie pie springs back when lightly pressed down. Cool on a rack for 30 minutes before filling. Store unfilled whoopie pies in a resealable container at room temperature or in the refrigerator for up to 3 days.

For the Filling

In a large bowl, cream butter with an electric mixer. Add vanilla. Gradually add sugar, beating well and scraping the sides of the bowl. Add mango nectar and beat until light and fluffy. Add freeze-dried mango and continue beating. Let stand at room temperature for 2 hours to let the mango flavor develop.

Store in the refrigerator until ready to fill the whoopie pies. If the filling gets too hard, let it sit out at room temperature until it's soft enough to pipe or spread. The filling can be stored in a resealable container in the refrigerator for up to 2 days.

See pages 8–10 for filling instructions.

1.

Assemble the whoopie pie (see pages 8–10 for instructions).

2.

With the rolling pin, flatten a large ball of green fondant on a sheet of parchment paper. With the sharp knife, cut the fondant in the shape of a leaf as shown.

3.

Use the knife to make indentations to create the leaf's veins as shown.

4.

Place the leaf on top of the whoopie pie.

5.

With orange fondant, roll a small ball to form the caterpillar's head.

6.

For the caterpillar's eyes, roll 2 tiny balls of white fondant, add teensy black fondant pupils, and then place the eyes on the head as shown.

7.

To create the nose, roll a tiny ball of pink fondant and place it under the eyes. To create the mouth, roll a tiny ball of red fondant. Apply it to the head and use a toothpick to make a hole in the center as shown.

8.

For the antennas, use black fondant to roll a thin sausage shape and cut it in half. Add a tiny ball of black fondant on the end of each half and apply the antennas to the head as shown.

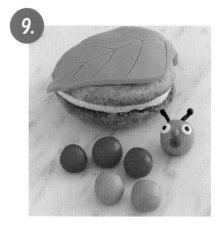

With orange fondant, roll 2 balls slightly smaller than the one used for the head. Then use red fondant to roll 3 more balls of the same size.

Put the balls together, alternating the colors as shown. Attach the head to the body and place the caterpillar on the leaf. Push the balls together slightly to arch the caterpillar's back as shown.

With This Ring . . .

Mocha Whoopie Pie with Cardamom Buttercream Filling

Two gold wedding rings on a whoopie pie — what a delicious way to seal a matrimonial vow! A perfect accompaniment to the wedding cake on someone's special day, these whoopie pies can also serve as lovely engagement-party favors.

Makes about 8–9 large whoopie pies or 16–18 small ones.

INGREDIENTS

For the Whoopie Pies

1 ½ cups all-purpose flour
1 teaspoon baking powder
¼ teaspoon salt
½ cup unsalted butter
2 3-ounce squares unsweetened chocolate, melted
4 tablespoons instant espresso powder
1 cup dark brown sugar, firmly packed

2 large eggs
2 teaspoons vanilla extract
1 cup sour cream

For the Filling

1 cup unsalted butter, softened
4 cups confectioners' sugar
1 teaspoon vanilla extract
2 teaspoons milk
2 teaspoons cardamom powder

Preheat oven to 350°F (180°C). Grease 2 cookie sheets with butter or cover them with parchment paper.

For the Whoopie Pies

In a medium bowl, mix together flour, baking powder, and salt. Set aside. Melt butter and chocolate together in a double boiler. Add espresso powder and stir well. In a large bowl, mix together the chocolate mixture and sugar. Add eggs and vanilla and mix well. Add sour cream and then stir in the flour mixture until just combined.

With a small ice-cream scoop or spoon, scoop the batter onto the cookie sheet, making sure to leave 3 inches between each whoopie. Bake in the center of the oven for about 12–14 minutes or until the top of a whoopie pie springs back when lightly pressed down. Cool on a rack for 30 minutes before filling. Store unfilled whoopie pies in a resealable container at room temperature or in the refrigerator for up to 3 days.

For the Filling

In a large bowl, cream butter with an electric mixer. Gradually add sugar, beating well and scraping the sides of the bowl. Add vanilla, milk, and cardamom and beat until light and fluffy. Store in the refrigerator until ready to fill the whoopie pies. If the filling gets too hard, let it sit out at room temperature until it's soft enough to pipe or spread. The filling can be stored in a resealable container in the refrigerator for up to 2 days.

See pages 8–10 for filling instructions.

1.

Assemble the whoopie pie (see pages 8–10 for instructions).

2.

With the rolling pin, flatten a large ball of red fondant on a sheet of parchment paper. Use the sharp knife to cut a circle slightly larger than the top of the whoopie pie and place it on top of the whoopie pie.

3. Use the rolling pin to roll out a thick piece of white fondant. Use the knife to cut it into a square as shown.

4. Press the sides or edges of the square with your finger to create a pillow.

5.

Use your finger to press in the center of the square as shown.

6.

With the knife, cut indentations extending from the center toward each corner as shown.

7.

Add a tiny ball of white fondant to the center and press down slightly.

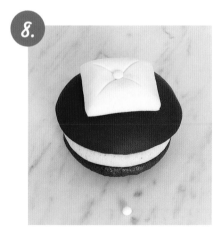

8.

Place the pillow on top of the whoopie pie.

9.

With gold fondant, roll a thin sausage shape. Flatten it and bring the ends together to form a ring.

10.

Create a second ring using the instructions above. Place the 2 rings on the pillow as shown.

Sweet Baby Dreams

Almond Whoopie Pie with Orange Buttercream Filling

It's hard to resist these adorable whoopie pies topped with pastel pacifiers. They are the perfect dessert or favor for a baby shower, or perhaps even a special "welcome home" treat for the new parents.

Makes about 9–10 large whoopie pies or 18–20 small ones.

INGREDIENTS

For the Whoopie Pies
2 cups all-purpose flour
1 1/2 teaspoons baking powder
1/4 teaspoon salt
1/2 cup unsalted butter,
  softened
1 1/2 cups sugar
1 large egg
2 teaspoons almond extract
3/4 cup buttermilk
1 cup almonds, finely ground

For the Filling
1 cup unsalted butter,
  softened
4 cups confectioners' sugar
1 teaspoon orange zest
4 tablespoons fresh-squeezed
  orange juice
2 teaspoons vanilla extract
2 tablespoons light corn syrup

Preheat oven to 350°F (180°C). Grease 2 cookie sheets with butter or cover them with parchment paper.

For the Whoopie Pies

In a medium bowl, mix together flour, baking powder, and salt. Set aside. In a large bowl, mix together butter and sugar. Add egg and almond extract and mix well. Add about half the flour mixture to the batter and then add buttermilk, and then the rest of the flour mixture. Fold in ground almonds.

With a small ice-cream scoop or spoon, scoop the batter onto the cookie sheet, making sure to leave 3 inches between each whoopie. Bake in the center of the oven for about 12–14 minutes or until the top of a whoopie pie springs back when lightly pressed down. Cool on a rack for 30 minutes before filling. Store unfilled whoopie pies in a resealable container at room temperature or in the refrigerator for up to 3 days.

For the Filling

In a large bowl, cream butter with an electric mixer. Gradually add sugar, beating well and scraping the sides of the bowl. Add orange zest, juice, vanilla, and light corn syrup and beat until light and fluffy. Store in the refrigerator until ready to fill the whoopie pies. If the filling gets too hard, let it sit out at room temperature until it's soft enough to pipe or spread. The filling can be stored in a resealable container in the refrigerator for up to 2 days.

See pages 8–10 for filling instructions.

You will need

- Fondant in the following colors: white, pale green, lavender, pale yellow
- Rolling pin
- Parchment paper
- Sharp knife

Assemble the whoopie pie (see pages 8–10 for instructions).

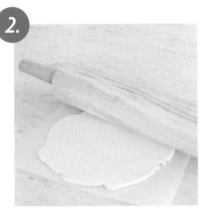

With the rolling pin, flatten a large ball of white fondant on a sheet of parchment paper.

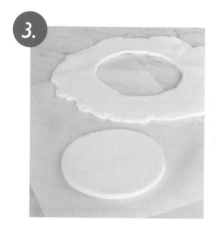

3. Use the sharp knife to cut a circle slightly larger than the top of the whoopie pie.

4. Place the fondant circle on top of the whoopie pie.

5.

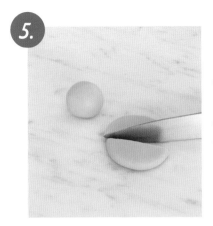

With pale-green fondant, roll medium ball and flatten it to form a circle. Cut the circle in half.

6.

Place one half of the circle in the middle of the whoopie pie as shown.

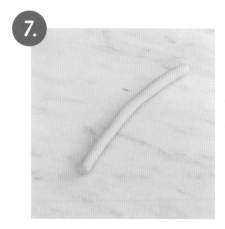

With lavender fondant, form a sausage shape about 3 inches in length.

Bring the ends together to form a ring and place it on the whoopie pie as shown.

9. With pale-yellow fondant, make a small ball and roll one end thinner to form the nipple part of the pacifier. Place it on the whoopie pie as shown.

10. With the remaining green, lavender, and yellow fondant, roll tiny balls, flatten them, and place them randomly around the white fondant as shown.

Monster and Co.

Blueberry Whoopie Pie with Pastry Cream Filling

No matter how hard he tries, this goofy little monster is anything but scary. Perched atop a yummy blueberry whoopie pie, this spotted fellow just cannot help but look cute!

Makes about 8–9 large whoopie pies or 16–18 small ones.

Please note that this recipe for pastry cream is thicker than most, as it needs to be firm enough to use as whoopie-pie filling.

INGREDIENTS

For the Whoopie Pies

2 cups all-purpose flour
1 teaspoon baking powder
$\frac{1}{2}$ teaspoon baking soda
Pinch of salt
$\frac{1}{2}$ teaspoon cinnamon
$\frac{1}{4}$ teaspoon freshly grated nutmeg
$\frac{1}{3}$ cup vegetable oil
1 cup light brown sugar, firmly packed
2 large eggs
1 teaspoon vanilla extract
$\frac{1}{2}$ cup sour cream
1 cup fresh or frozen and defrosted blueberries

For the Filling

1 cup sugar
6 large egg yolks
$\frac{1}{2}$ cup cornstarch
1 cup milk
1 cup heavy cream
2 teaspoons vanilla extract

Preheat oven to 350°F (180°C). Grease 2 cookie sheets with butter or cover them with parchment paper.

For the Whoopie Pies

In a medium bowl, mix together flour, baking powder, baking soda, salt, cinnamon, and nutmeg. Set aside. In a large bowl, mix together oil and sugar. Add eggs and vanilla and mix well. Add sour cream and then stir in the flour mixture until just combined. Gently fold blueberries into the batter.

With a small ice-cream scoop or spoon, scoop the batter onto the cookie sheet, making sure to leave 3 inches between each whoopie. Bake in the center of the oven for about 12–14 minutes or until the top of a whoopie pie springs back when lightly pressed down. Cool on a rack for 30 minutes before filling. Store unfilled whoopie pies in a resealable container at room temperature or in the refrigerator for up to 3 days.

For the Filling

In a medium bowl, beat together sugar and egg yolks. Add cornstarch and mix well. Place milk and cream in a saucepan and bring to a simmer. Carefully pour ⅓ of the hot milk mixture into the egg mixture and stir until smooth. Add the rest of the liquid and mix. Pour the mixture back into the saucepan and place on the stove over medium heat. Slowly bring to a boil, mixing with a wooden spoon. The cream will gradually thicken. Turn off the heat and add vanilla, mixing until smooth. Transfer to a medium-sized bowl and place a piece of plastic wrap on the surface of the cream so a crust doesn't form. Chill in the refrigerator until ready to use.

The filling can be stored in a resealable container in the refrigerator for up to 2 days. See pages 8–10 for filling instructions.

- Fondant in the following colors: purple, blue, pink, white, black
- Rolling pin
- Parchment paper
- Sharp knife

1.

Assemble the whoopie pie (see pages 8–10 for instructions).

2.

With the rolling pin, flatten a large ball of purple fondant on a sheet of parchment paper. Use the sharp knife to cut a circle slightly larger than the top of the whoopie pie and place it on top of the whoopie pie.

3.

With blue fondant, form a medium-sized ball. Flatten the ball as shown and place it in the center of the whoopie pie.

4.

For the tongue, use pink fondant to form a small sausage shape and flatten it. Use the knife to create an indentation in the middle and place it on the blue circle as shown.

5. With blue fondant, roll a medium-sized ball and flatten 1 side to create a half sphere. Apply it to the top of the whoopie pie as shown.

6. With white fondant, roll 2 tiny balls for the eyes. Add teensy black fondant dots for pupils and place the eyes on the monster's head.

7.

With pink fondant, create eyelids. Roll a small ball of pink fondant, flatten it, and cut it in half to form the eyelids. Place each half on an eye as shown.

8.

With purple fondant, form 2 small cones.

9.

Place the cones on top of the head as shown.

10.

With purple fondant, create teensy spots, flatten them, and place them on the head as shown.

Flower Power

Peanut Butter Whoopie Pie with Milk Chocolate Ganache Filling

Welcome to a super delicious garden where the edible flowers look almost too good to eat. But who could resist the classic peanut-butter-and-chocolate whoopie pie beneath? These make a terrific addition to a Mother's Day celebration.

Makes about 8–9 large whoopie pies or 16–18 small ones.

INGREDIENTS

For the Whoopie Pies

1 ½ cups all-purpose flour
2 teaspoons baking powder
¼ teaspoon salt
½ cup unsalted butter, softened
1 cup light brown sugar, firmly packed
½ cup peanut butter
½ cup Nutella
2 large eggs
1 teaspoon vanilla extract
1 cup sour cream

For the Filling

8 ounces milk chocolate, finely chopped
½ cup heavy cream

Preheat oven to 350°F (180°C). Grease 2 cookie sheets with butter or cover them with parchment paper.

For the Whoopie Pies

In a medium bowl, mix together flour, baking powder, and salt. Set aside. In a large bowl, mix together butter and sugar. Add peanut butter, Nutella, eggs, and vanilla and mix well. Add sour cream and then stir in the flour mixture until just combined.

With a small ice-cream scoop or spoon, scoop the batter onto the cookie sheet, making sure to leave 3 inches between each whoopie. Bake in the center of the oven for about 12 –14 minutes or until the top of a whoopie pie springs back when lightly pressed down. Cool on a rack for 30 minutes before filling. Store unfilled whoopie pies in a resealable container at room temperature or in the refrigerator for up to 3 days.

For the Filling

Place chopped chocolate in a medium-sized bowl. In a small saucepan, bring cream to a near boil. Pour the hot cream over the chocolate and stir until smooth. The filling will thicken as it cools.

Store in the refrigerator until ready to fill the whoopie pies. If the filling gets too hard, let it sit out at room temperature until it's soft enough to pipe or spread. The filling can be stored in a resealable container in the refrigerator for up to 2 days.

See pages 8–10 for filling instructions.

1.

Assemble the whoopie pie (see pages 8–10 for instructions).

2.

With the rolling pin, flatten a large ball of brown fondant on a sheet of parchment paper. Use the sharp knife cut to a circle slightly larger than the top of the whoopie pie and place it on top of the whoopie pie.

3.

With green fondant, form a small ball. Roll the ends thin as shown and flatten the fondant to form a leaf shape.

4.

Use the knife to make indentations to create the veins. Make 2 more leaves and place all 3 leaves on top of the whoopie pie, posing them as shown.

5.

Roll 5 small identical white balls and 1 yellow one.

6.

Use your fingers to flatten the balls and arrange the white ones in a circle. They should be touching slightly. Place the yellow ball in the middle and gently press down.

Carefully lift the flower and place it in the center of the leaves.

8.

To create another kind of flower, roll 5 small balls of red fondant into oval shapes and use your finger to flatten them into petals.

9.

To create the center of the flower or pistil, take some pink fondant and make a small oval shape. Use the knife to make 4 slits as shown. Roll a tiny ball of white fondant and place it in the center of the pistil.

10.

Arrange the flattened red petals in a circle, touching slightly. Place the pistil in the middle and carefully set the flower on the leaves as shown.

Funny Faces

Orange Whoopie Pie with Chocolate Buttercream Filling

What fun the kids will have making different faces out of fondant! They can make a simple self-portrait or compete to make the silliest face. The possibilities are endless.

Makes about 8–9 large whoopie pies or 16–18 small ones.

INGREDIENTS

For the Whoopie Pies

2 cups all-purpose flour
$1/2$ teaspoon baking soda
1 teaspoon baking powder
Pinch of salt
$1/2$ cup unsalted butter, softened
1 cup sugar
2 large eggs
2 teaspoons orange zest
$1/3$ cup orange juice concentrate, thawed

For the Filling

1 cup unsalted butter, softened
3 cups confectioners' sugar
6 tablespoons cocoa powder
2 teaspoons milk
1 teaspoon vanilla extract (or Grand Marnier)
2 tablespoons light corn syrup

Preheat oven to 350°F (180°C). Grease 2 cookie sheets with butter or cover them with parchment paper.

For the Whoopie Pies

In a medium bowl, mix together flour, baking soda, baking powder, and salt. Set aside. In a large bowl, cream butter and sugar with an electric mixer until light and fluffy. Add one egg at a time, mixing well after each addition. Add orange zest and orange juice concentrate. Stir in the flour mixture until just combined.

With a small ice-cream scoop or spoon, scoop the batter onto the cookie sheet, making sure to leave 3 inches between each whoopie. Bake in the center of the oven for about 12–14 minutes or until the top of a whoopie pie springs back when lightly pressed down. Cool on a rack for 30 minutes before filling. Store unfilled whoopie pies in a resealable container at room temperature or in the refrigerator for up to 3 days.

For the Filling

In a large bowl, cream butter with an electric mixer. Gradually add sugar and cocoa powder, beating well and scraping the sides of the bowl. Slowly add milk and vanilla (or Grand Marnier) and beat until light and fluffy.

Store in the refrigerator until ready to fill the whoopie pies. If the filling gets too hard, let it sit out at room temperature until it's soft enough to pipe or spread. The filling can be stored in a resealable container in the refrigerator for up to 2 days.

See pages 8–10 for filling instructions.

You will need

- Fondant in the following colors: flesh (various shades), yellow, red, green, white, black, pink, brown
- Rolling pin
- Parchment paper
- Sharp knife
- Toothpick

Assemble the whoopie pie (see pages 8–10 for instructions).

With the rolling pin, flatten a large ball of flesh-colored fondant on a sheet of parchment paper. Use the sharp knife to cut a circle slightly larger than the top of the whoopie pie and place it on top of the whoopie pie.

3.

To make the boy's hair, roll out a strip of yellow fondant. Use the knife to cut out a long rectangle as shown (about the diameter of the whoopie pie in length). Make an indentation in the middle of the rectangle. Make slits to create the strands of hair. Place the hair on the head as shown.

4.

To make the girl's hair, roll out a strip of red fondant and use the knife to cut a longer rectangle (about double the length of the rectangle in step 3). Make the same indentation and slits as described in step 3. After placing the hair on the head, press together the strands to form pigtails. Press a little green ball of fondant to each pigtail as shown.

5.

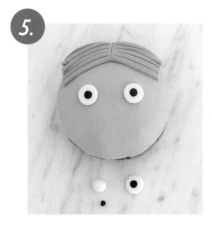

For the eyes, roll 2 small balls of white fondant. Flatten them and add 2 teensy, flattened black fondant dots for pupils. Place the eyes on the head.

6.

To create the eyelids, roll a small ball of flesh-colored fondant, flatten it to form a circle, and use the knife to cut it in half. Apply the lids to the eyes as shown.

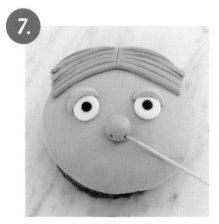

For the nose, roll a small ball of flesh-colored fondant. Place it on the face and use the toothpick to create nostrils as shown.

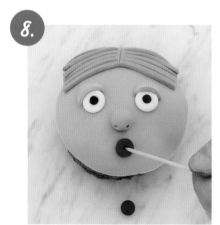

For the mouth, roll a small ball of red fondant, slightly flatten it, and apply it to the face. Use the toothpick to create a hole as shown.

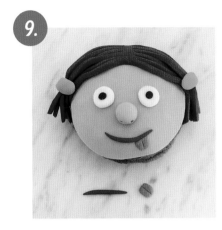

9. For an alternative to the mouth described in step 8, roll a thin sausage shape with red fondant. Apply it to the face, shaping it to create the desired facial expression. If you would like to add a tongue, take a small amount of pink fondant and create a sausage shape. Flatten it and use the knife to make an indentation in the middle. Place it on the face as shown.

10. To make the faces more interesting, you can add freckles (use teensy dots of brown fondant), rosy cheeks (add 2 identical red flattened balls to the cheeks), or eyebrows (use the same color fondant as used for the hair to make little strips, and apply them above the eyes).

Holiday Stockings

Gingerbread Whoopie Pie with Mascarpone Filling

A festive way to celebrate a holiday party, whether it's Christmas, Hanukkah, or Kwanzaa, these whoopie pies festooned with colorful stockings feature a favorite seasonal flavor. So easy to make and so delicious to eat!

Makes about 8–9 large whoopie pies or 16–18 small ones.

INGREDIENTS

For the Whoopie Pies

2 cups all-purpose flour

2 teaspoons baking powder

$1/4$ teaspoon salt

$1/2$ cup unsalted butter, softened

1 cup light brown sugar, firmly packed

$1/2$ cup molasses

2 large eggs

2 teaspoons ground ginger

1 teaspoon cinnamon

1 teaspoon vanilla extract

$1/2$ cup sour cream

$1/4$ cup candied ginger, finely chopped

For the Filling

$1 1/2$ cups confectioners' sugar

6 tablespoons unsalted butter, softened

$1/2$ cup mascarpone

$1/2$ teaspoon vanilla extract

Preheat oven to 350°F (180°C). Grease 2 cookie sheets with butter or cover them with parchment paper.

For the Whoopie Pies

In a medium bowl, mix together flour, baking powder, and salt. Set aside. In a large bowl, mix together butter and sugar. Add molasses, eggs, ground ginger, cinnamon, and vanilla and mix well. Add sour cream and then stir in the flour mixture until just combined. Fold in chopped candied ginger.

With a small ice-cream scoop or spoon, scoop the batter onto the cookie sheet, making sure to leave 3 inches between each whoopie. Bake in the center of the oven for about 12 – 14 minutes or until the top of a whoopie pie springs back when lightly pressed down. Cool on a rack for 30 minutes before filling. Store unfilled whoopie pies in a resealable container at room temperature or in the refrigerator for up to 3 days.

For the Filling

In a large bowl, cream sugar and butter with an electric mixer on medium speed until light and fluffy. Add mascarpone and vanilla and stir until smooth.

Store in the refrigerator until ready to fill the whoopie pies. If the filling gets too hard, let it sit out at room temperature until it's soft enough to pipe or spread. The filling can be stored in a resealable container in the refrigerator for up to 2 days.

See pages 8–10 for filling instructions.

- Fondant in the following colors: green, red, white
- Rolling pin
- Parchment paper
- Sharp knife

1.

Assemble the whoopie pie (see pages 8–10 for instructions).

2.

With the rolling pin, flatten a large ball of green fondant on a sheet of parchment paper. Use the sharp knife to cut a circle slightly larger than the top of the whoopie pie and place it on top of the whoopie pie.

3.

To create the stocking, use red fondant to make a sausage shape about 3 inches in length.

4.

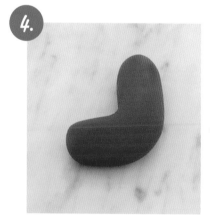

Bend the sausage at an angle to create the stocking.

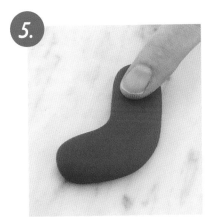

5. Flatten the stocking slightly.

6. With a small amount of white fondant, make a sausage shape about 2 inches in length and flatten it. Wrap it around the top of the stocking as shown.

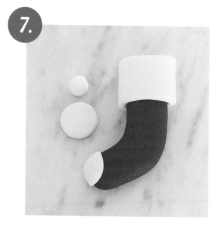

7.

With a small amount of white fondant, make a ball, flatten it to make a circle, and press it around the toe as shown.

8.

Repeat step 7 to create another patch and press it around the heel as shown.

9.

With red fondant, create a thin strip, bend it, and attach it to the top as shown.

10.

If desired, roll teensy balls of green fondant, flatten them, and place them on the stocking in a random manner. Place the stocking on the whoopie pie.

Table of Equivalents

Some of the conversions in these lists have been slightly rounded for measuring convenience.

VOLUME:

U.S.	metric
¼ teaspoon	1.25 milliliters
½ teaspoon	2.5 milliliters
¾ teaspoon	3.75 milliliters
1 teaspoon	5 milliliters
1 tablespoon (3 teaspoons)	15 milliliters
2 tablespoons	30 milliliters
3 tablespoons	45 milliliters
1 fluid ounce (2 tablespoons)	30 milliliters
¼ cup (4 tablespoons)	60 milliliters
⅓ cup	80 milliliters
½ cup	120 milliliters
⅔ cup	160 milliliters
1 cup	240 milliliters
2 cups (1 pint)	480 milliliters
4 cups (1 quart or 32 ounces)	960 milliliters
1 gallon (4 quarts)	3.8 liters

OVEN TEMPERATURE:

fahrenheit	celsius
250	120
275	140
300	150
325	160
350	180
375	190
400	200
425	220
450	230
475	240
500	260

WEIGHT:

U.S.	metric
1 ounce (by weight)	28 grams
1 pound	448 grams
2.2 pounds	1 kilogram

LENGTH:

U.S.	metric
⅛ inch	3 millimeters
¼ inch	6 millimeters
½ inch	12 millimeters
1 inch	2.5 centimeters